W9-BBR-650

SUPERSTARS
of
PRO FOOTBALL

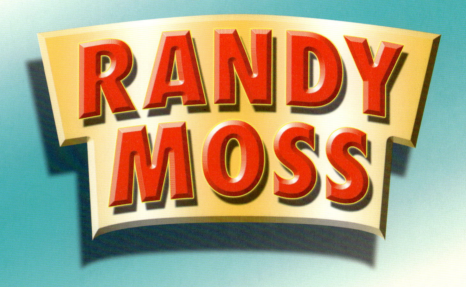

RANDY MOSS

David Robson

Mason Crest Publishers

Produced by OTTN Publishing in association with
21st Century Publishing and Communications, Inc.

MASON CREST PUBLISHERS INC.
370 Reed Road
Broomall, Pennsylvania 19008
(866) MCP-BOOK (toll free)
www.masoncrest.com

Printed in the United States of America.

First Printing

9 8 7 6 5 4 3 2 1

Library of Congress Cataloging-in-Publication Data

Robson, David, 1966–
    Randy Moss / David Robson.
        p. cm. — (Superstars of pro football)
    ISBN 978-1-4222-0550-1 (hardcover) — ISBN 978-1-4222-0830-4 (pbk.)
    1. Moss, Randy—Juvenile literature. 2. Football players—United States—
Biography—Juvenile literature. I. Title.
GV939.M67R63 2008
796.332092—dc22
[B]   2008029822

Publisher's note:
All quotations in this book come from original sources, and contain the spelling
and grammatical inconsistencies of the original text.

◀◀ CROSS-CURRENTS ▶▶

In the ebb and flow of the currents of life we are each influenced
by many people, places, and events that we directly experience or
have learned about. Throughout the chapters of this book you will
come across CROSS-CURRENTS reference bubbles. These bubbles
direct you to a CROSS-CURRENTS section in the back of the
book that contains fascinating and informative sidebars
and related pictures. Go on. ▶▶

◄◄CONTENTS►►

DOWN BUT NOT OUT

The statement from the New England Patriots was brief and to the point: All-Pro **wide receiver** Randy Moss and star quarterback Tom Brady would not play in the 2008 Pro Bowl in Honolulu, Hawaii. After a bruising defeat to the New York Giants in Super Bowl XLII, Moss and Brady were staying home.

According to the Patriots, Brady and Moss were suffering from ankle injuries. The announcement quietly ended a season that had been anything but quiet. In the months leading up to their Super Bowl appearance, the Patriots had destroyed the competition, ending the regular season with an undefeated record of 16–0.

Members of the New England Patriots' offensive unit, including quarterback Tom Brady (left) and wide receiver Randy Moss (second from left), celebrate a touchdown against the Buffalo Bills, September 23, 2007. The Patriots won the game, 38–7.

For over a year, the Patriots and their intense head coach Bill Belichick had been determined to make it back to the Super Bowl. The off-season signing of Moss, one of the best wide receivers in the National Football League (NFL), only added to the team's dazzling array of offensive weapons. For his part, Moss delighted in the idea of joining a team that had won three Super Bowls during the 2000s. The Patriots seemed to be on their way to another glorious championship, and Moss had done his share in getting them there.

The Patriots were known as a team whose members were willing to sacrifice individual

CROSS-CURRENTS

Read "Coach Belichick" to learn more about the influential and respected coach of the New England Patriots. Go to page 46. ▶▶

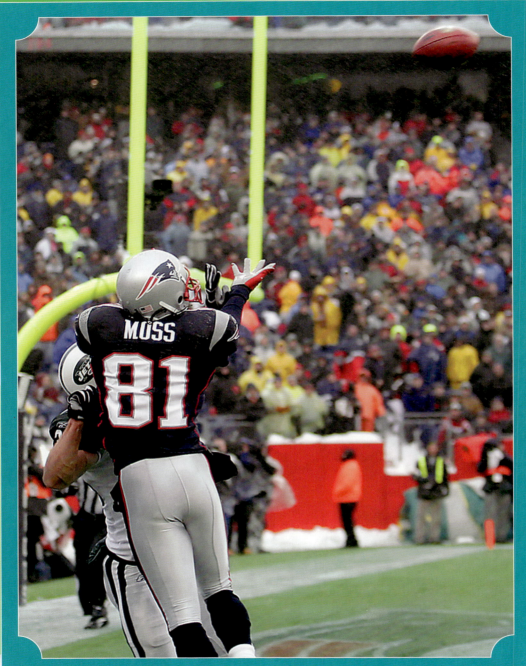

Randy Moss is well covered as he leaps for a Tom Brady pass in a game against the New York Jets, December 16, 2007. The Patriots won the game, 20–10, to boost their record to 14–0.

glory for the good of the team. At the beginning of the 2007 season, a successful pairing of the unpredictable Moss and the reliable Patriots had seemed unlikely.

Ups and Downs

During much of his nine-year career, Randy Moss made headlines both on and off the field. He was one of the highest-paid players in the game, and his **gridiron** exploits were legendary. But there was also another side to Moss. Over the years, Moss earned a reputation as being conceited, selfish, and bad-tempered. As a Viking, Moss had once squirted an official with water during a playoff game and then left the field early. In two seasons with Oakland, the once high-flying receiver remained virtually grounded. He was often injured and angry. Thus Moss remained a mystery to many players and fans. While his one-handed grabs and acrobatic moves were beyond criticism, there had often been rumblings about whether Moss was a team player or just in it for his own personal gain.

With the Patriots it would be different, Moss assured Coach Belichick. The Patriots, cautious at first, were glad to have him. They traded the Raiders a fourth-round **draft** pick for the 31-year-old receiver, whom they believed had at least one more outstanding year in him. Belichick knew the risks, as did team owner Robert Kraft. But, says Kraft, he listened when Moss approached him:

> **"In this case, he came to us and wanted to be part of a team that could win and he said to me: 'Mr. Kraft, I have made a lot of money, more money probably than I need. This is about winning.' He lived up to every commitment he has made, and he also treats people very well in this organization. Everything that I've seen, he has conducted himself very well."**

Patriot Power

The 2007 season with the Patriots had gone almost flawlessly for Moss. There had been no temper tantrums or on-the-field misbehavior. Moss had shown no resentment when quarterback Tom Brady spread the ball around to other receivers. During games, at least, it appeared that Moss was a new man, older and wiser. Off the

Randy Moss speaks to reporters on Super Bowl XLII Media Day, January 29, 2007. "Before I retired," Moss said, "I wanted to have a chance to play on this stage."

field, however, sportswriters saw the same old Randy Moss. During the playoffs, a woman told authorities that Moss had assaulted her. Moss denied the accusation and said the woman was trying to squeeze him for money.

Still, despite personal challenges, Moss kept showing up for games ready to play. By the time the Patriots reached Super Bowl XLII, they were picked to beat the New York Giants by 12 points. The Giants, a scrappy **wild-card** team, looked as surprised as anyone that they had made it so far. Moss, for one, couldn't wait for the big day:

> **"Before I retired, I wanted to have a chance to play on this stage, not for all the publicity and everything but just playing in the Super Bowl. I mean, you hear about a lot of greats and a lot of guys making their name as Super Bowl MVPs and being able to win the big game. So that's what I wanted. I wanted to be on this stage to play the big game, the last game of the season."**

But from the opening kickoff, things did not go as planned for the Patriots. The team struggled for much of the game. Yet, despite mistakes, by the fourth quarter it remained New England's game to win. The strong arm of Tom Brady and the Patriots' sturdy defense kept them in the game.

So, too, did Randy Moss's five **receptions** and touchdown catch. But a last-minute **drive** by the Giants and their quarterback Eli Manning dashed the Patriots' hopes. The scoreboard told the tale: New York Giants 17, New England Patriots 14. Super Bowl XLII would go down as one of the biggest upsets in sports history.

CROSS-CURRENTS

If you would like to find out about the history of Randy Moss's team, check out "The New England Patriots." Go to page 48. ▶▶

After the game, Moss stood stunned, his helmet hanging limply by his side. He knew the sting of defeat from past experience, but it had never felt quite like this. He'd signed a one-year **contract** with the Patriots and had no idea whether he'd ever get another chance to win a Super Bowl. As the seconds wound down at Super Bowl XLII, many wondered what the next move in Randy Moss's unpredictable career would be.

TROUBLED TALENT

Randall Gene Moss was born in Rand, West Virginia, on February 13, 1977. His mother, Maxine, raised Randy along with his sister, Lutisia, and brother, Eric. As a single parent, Maxine had a hard time supporting her family. What got the family through, says Moss, was their faith in God and Maxine's dedication to her children:

"After God is my mother, 'cause she had me, she raised me, and she kept clothes on my back, kept a roof over my head. . . . My mom worked two and three jobs to try and support me and my sister and brother. . . . I never forget where I came from and how I was brought up. I consider myself really blessed."

This house in Rand, West Virginia, was the childhood home of Randy Moss. He and his brother and sister were raised by a single mother who often worked two jobs to support the family.

As a young man, Moss dreamed of one day playing football for the University of Notre Dame in Indiana, which has a legendary football program. Moss also thought about playing for Ohio State, where his brother Eric once played. However, his heart belonged to the Fighting Irish at Notre Dame. He worked hard both on the field and in the classroom to achieve his dream.

Fighting Irish

In 1995 Moss signed a letter of intent with Notre Dame. This said that once his playing days at DuPont High School in West Virginia were finished, the university would offer him a place on its football team. At six foot four and

CROSS-CURRENTS

To learn more about the tradition of football at the University of Notre Dame, read "Notre Dame: A Proud Football History." Go to page 49. ▶▶

200 pounds, Moss was a star player during his high school years. He led DuPont to two state titles—returning kicks, punting, and playing defensive back. As a senior he was named high school player of the year in both football and basketball.

But already a less attractive side of the young athlete was showing through. Moss was often short-tempered and angry. He was involved in several fights in school and was once suspended for his actions. The most serious incident occurred when Moss attacked a student he believed was a racist. The victim ended up in the hospital with injuries to his head, kidney, and spleen. Moss was arrested.

In court Moss pleaded guilty to the attack and received probation and a 30-day jail sentence. He was also forced to look elsewhere for athletic opportunity. His Notre Dame dream fell apart when the university learned about his legal troubles and withdrew its **scholarship** offer. But the talented player soon received another offer, this one from Florida State University. The Seminoles' head coach, Bobby Bowden, had dealt with difficult players before. Bowden was convinced that he could help Moss.

In the meantime, law enforcement officials agreed to allow Moss to spend three days in jail before the start of the football season, and finish the remaining 27 days of his sentence after the season ended. But even this was controversial. Some in the press suggested that the talented young athlete was receiving special treatment. Jim Fout, Moss's high school baseball coach, disagreed:

> **"It was a bad scene. What Randy did was wrong. He knows that. But if it had been just another student in the school and not Randy Moss, it never would have become what it did. The student would have been disciplined, for sure, but that prosecuting attorney, once he heard it was Moss, he was going after him."**

Another Chance

In the end it made little difference, as Moss was not able to join the Seminoles after all. Because he had signed the letter of intent with Notre Dame, the National Collegiate Athletic Association (NCAA)

During his youth, Randy Moss got into more than his share of trouble. In high school, his beating of a fellow student resulted in a 30-day jail sentence—and ended his dream of playing football at the University of Notre Dame.

labeled Moss a transfer student. The NCAA ruled that he could not play for Florida State in 1995. His football career would have to wait.

The wait became even longer when Moss, serving his 30-day jail sentence, failed a drug test. This violated his probation. For Florida State this was the final straw. The university withdrew its scholarship offer. Moss remained in jail, serving an additional 60 days behind bars for his probation violation.

But a silver lining soon appeared in Moss's cloudy future, this time close to home. West Virginia's Marshall University, an hour's

The Marshall University band performs during halftime of a home football game. Randy Moss was a star on Marshall's football team, helping lead the Thundering Herd to a Division I-AA football championship in 1996.

drive from Moss's hometown of Rand, decided to take a chance on him. Moss made the most of his opportunity. In 1996 he set the Division I-AA records for most games with a touchdown (14) and most consecutive games with a touchdown catch (13). Moss seemed to do it all, also returning kickoffs for a total of 484 yards and a 34.6-yard average. Thanks in part to Moss's hard work, Marshall went undefeated and won the Division I-AA championship. During his second year at Marshall, Moss and Marshall quarterback Chad Pennington teamed up to clinch the Mid-American conference title.

The Marshall Plan

Moss's time at Marshall was not without controversy. In 1997 the sophomore spoke about a tragic 1970 plane crash that had killed a dozen Marshall football players and coaches. He said that while the crash had been tragic, it was no big deal to him. Later, Moss claimed his words had been taken out of context. However, many Marshall fans were upset by the insensitive remarks. But with 25 touchdown catches during the 1997 season and talk of a possible Heisman Trophy win, Moss still attracted the attention of NFL teams.

Although Moss did not win the Heisman that year, he hoped that professional football teams would soon be calling. In the 1998 NFL draft, Moss attracted plenty of interest, although some teams were hesitant to choose an apparently troubled young football player. But the Minnesota Vikings decided to gamble. In the end Moss was the 21st player chosen in 1998.

CROSS-CURRENTS

To learn more about the most prestigious award given to college football players, read "The Heisman Trophy." Go to page 50. ▶▶

SEEING PURPLE

In the NFL, most **rookie** wide receivers need a year or two before they are ready to play regularly. The defenses are better at the professional level, and this makes it harder for receivers to catch the ball. However, Moss made an immediate impact for the Vikings in 1998. In his first regular-season game, he caught two touchdown passes.

During the 1998 season, Minnesota had the league's best offense. Moss teamed up with a pair of veteran receivers, Cris Carter and Jake Reed. They gave quarterback Randall Cunningham three big, fast targets. Cunningham had his best season ever, throwing 34 touchdown passes. The team had other offensive stars as well. Running back Robert Smith gained nearly 1,200 yards

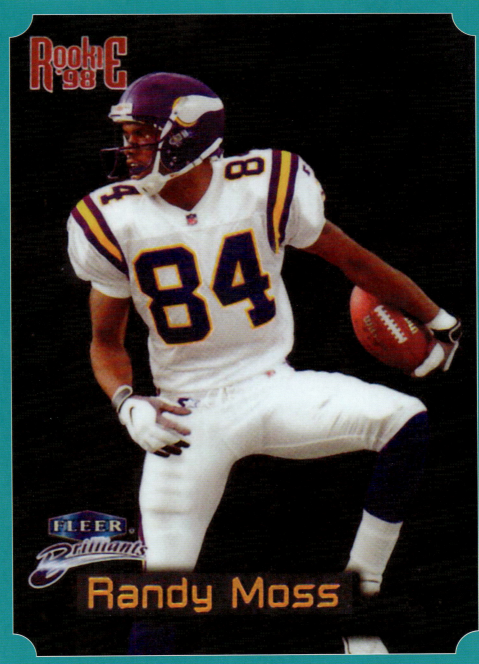

A Randy Moss rookie card. Even though the 1998 Minnesota Vikings had an arsenal of offensive weapons, Moss stood out. He notched a league-leading 17 touchdown receptions during the season.

on the ground. Gary Anderson became the first kicker in NFL history not to miss a field goal or extra point during a season. Overall, the Vikings set an NFL record by scoring 556 points in the 1998 season. They finished with a 15–1 record.

Many people expected that the Vikings would reach the Super Bowl. But Minnesota suffered a stunning overtime loss in the National Football Conference (NFC) Championship game to the Atlanta Falcons.

Randy Moss runs away from Detroit Lions cornerback Robert Bailey, September 20, 1998. Big, strong, and fast, Moss was a difficult receiver to cover, particularly as defenses also had to worry about Minnesota's other outstanding receivers, Cris Carter and Jake Reed.

Moss was named to the Pro Bowl after the 1998 season. He also received the NFL's Offensive Rookie of the Year award. Moss had caught 69 passes for 1,313 yards, the third-best yardage in the NFL. He also led the league with 17 touchdown catches.

Vikings coach Dennis Green had high praise for his young star. The coach compared Moss to one of the greatest receivers in NFL history: Jerry Rice, whom Green had coached in San Francisco. He told *Sport* magazine,

CROSS-CURRENTS

Read "The Pro Bowl" if you'd like to learn more about the National Football League's annual all-star game. Go to page 51. ▶▶

> **"I saw in Randy in his first year what I saw in Jerry Rice. . . . Jerry clearly wanted to be the best receiver who ever played the game—that was part of his mindset. I see that same thing in Randy, that desire to be the best, to really perform and just go out and play football."**

The Playoff Hunt

The next season, 1999, Randy Moss caught 80 passes for 1,413 yards and scored 11 touchdowns. Sportswriters and fans raved about Moss's terrific ability on the football field. But they also noticed his attitude. In a November game, Moss's past history of bad behavior reappeared. Moss got into trouble for yelling at a referee, and the National Football League fined him $10,000.

CROSS-CURRENTS

To learn more about Randy Moss's head coach in Minnesota, check out "Head Coach Dennis Green." Go to page 52. ▶▶

By the end of the 1999 season, the Vikings were back in the championship hunt again. They played the Dallas Cowboys in the NFC wild-card playoff game. Moss did his part by catching five passes for 127 yards. Their 27–10 win gave Minnesota a chance to challenge the mighty St. Louis Rams in an NFC divisional playoff game.

Early on, this playoff game became a shoot-out. The Vikings' defense could not stop Rams quarterback Kurt Warner from reaching the end zone. Moss's nine-catch, two-touchdown, 188-yard game was simply not enough. Despite a tough fight, the Vikings fell to the Rams, 49–37.

Randy Moss jumps over the back of a defender to pull in a pass during the Pro Bowl, Honolulu, Hawaii, February 6, 2000. Moss was picked for the Pro Bowl in each of his first three seasons in the NFL.

Moss got into trouble with the league again after the playoff game. During the fourth quarter, Moss grew angry after missing a pass. He squirted a referee with water. After the game, the NFL fined Moss $40,000. The fine was later reduced to $25,000, but there was a catch. If Moss violated league rules again, he would have to pay the additional $15,000.

The Vikings' 2000 season got off to a good start. Throughout most of the season, the men in purple ran up the score against their opponents. Thanks in large part to Randy Moss, Minnesota had one of the NFL's top offenses. The Vikings dominated offensively and had an 11–2 record through 13 weeks of play. Although the Vikings lost their last three games of the regular season—to the Rams, Green Bay Packers, and Indianapolis Colts—the team's playoff hopes were high. It was their fifth straight **postseason** appearance under head coach Dennis Green. To many sports fans it seemed like 2000 could finally be the team's championship year.

Moss had another great season in 2000. He teamed up with rookie quarterback Daunte Culpepper to score 15 touchdowns. For the second time in three years, Moss led the league in that category. Moss also broke a team record by gaining over 100 yards receiving in eight games. During one game, against Detroit in October, he grabbed seven passes for 168 yards. His strong season earned Moss a third trip to the Pro Bowl.

Victory and Disappointment

In the first round of the playoffs, the Vikings crushed the New Orleans Saints, 34 to 16. Moss scored two touchdowns and gained 121 yards. Afterward, some people were saying that the Vikings looked ready for the Super Bowl.

Next, the Minnesota team flew to the Meadowlands in New Jersey to face the New York Giants in the NFC Championship game. Although it was an away game for the Vikings, the oddsmakers picked Minnesota to win the game.

Minnesota fans were looking for another blowout. They got one—but it was the mighty Vikings who took the fall. The Giants kept a tight lid on Moss and running back Robert Smith, and trounced the Vikings, 41–0. It was the worst loss in team history.

After the season the team's future direction seemed uncertain. Although Smith had been the NFC's leading running back in 2000, gaining 1,521 yards, he decided to retire at the end of the season. The Vikings also faced the possibility of losing another key part of their offense. Randy Moss was in the final year of his contract. As the 2000 season came to a crashing finish, many Vikings fans wondered whether he would return.

A Man in Demand

The Vikings wanted Moss back. The talented receiver considered becoming a **free agent**. This would allow another team to offer him a large contract. However, in July 2001, after a long period of **negotiation**, he decided to stay in Minnesota. Moss signed an eight-year, $75 million contract with the Vikings. This made him the highest-paid player in NFL history.

Moss had earned this huge contract with his great performance on the field. In his first three seasons with the Vikings, he had caught 226 passes for 4,163 yards and an amazing 43 touchdowns. Those statistics were among the best in NFL history for a player's first three years. Moss told reporters that he was very happy about the new contract:

> **"I've been waiting on this day for a long time and it's finally here. Now I can concentrate on one thing and that's football. Security for me and my family is here. . . . I would like to give a big thanks to God for making me and my talents and name stand out and for keeping me healthy so I can be in this position."**

Typically, NFL players make the most money at the end of their contracts. If a player underperforms or doesn't satisfy the team for other reasons, that team can cut or trade the player. This can save the team a great deal of money. Randy, however, received a lot of money at the start of his deal. The star wide receiver pocketed $18 million over the first 19 months of the contract.

Despite the big off-season signing, the Vikings' 2001 season was a bust. Minnesota struggled all season long, finishing with a record of 5–11. Randy Moss played well in 2001, although his numbers were not as good as they had been in the past. He caught 82 passes for 1,233 yards and 10 touchdowns, putting him among the league's top receivers in all three categories. Still, Minnesota's streak of five playoff appearances in a row had ended.

Top Change and Trouble

The end of the 2001 season marked the end of the road for Vikings head coach Dennis Green. Mike Tice, a former tight end for the Vikings, replaced him. Tice became head coach for the last game of the 2001 season, a loss to the Baltimore Ravens.

Tice brought a change of attitude to the Vikings, but that did not immediately change the team's fortunes. Moss continued racking up solid statistics. He caught a career-high 106 passes for 1,347 yards in 2002, although he scored just seven touchdowns. The numbers were good enough to earn Moss a fourth invitation to the Pro Bowl. However, the Vikings finished with another losing record, at six wins and ten losses.

During the 2000 off-season, the Minnesota Vikings signed Randy Moss to a new eight-year, $75 million contract. At the time, it was the biggest contract in NFL history.

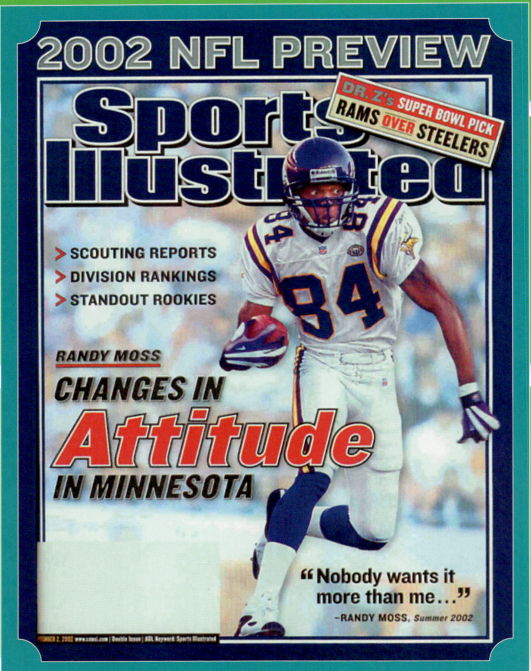

2002 NFL PREVIEW

DR. Z's SUPER BOWL PICK
RAMS OVER STEELERS

Sports Illustrated

> SCOUTING REPORTS
> DIVISION RANKINGS
> STANDOUT ROOKIES

RANDY MOSS

CHANGES IN

Attitude

IN MINNESOTA

" Nobody wants it more than me..."
–RANDY MOSS, *Summer 2002*

The cover of *Sports Illustrated* magazine's 2002 NFL preview issue featured a picture of Randy Moss. It also referred to changes in Minnesota, which had a new head coach, Mike Tice.

During the 2002 season, Moss found himself in legal trouble once again. One evening, Moss was about to make an illegal turn while driving in Minneapolis. A female traffic officer stood in front of his car and told him to stop. Moss bumped the officer with his vehicle. The officer fell over, and Moss was arrested. During a vehicle search, law enforcement officials found marijuana in the car. Moss was charged with assault for hitting the officer, as well as possession of illegal drugs. Eventually, the charges were dropped. In return, Moss pleaded guilty to a minor traffic violation. He completed 40 hours of community service and paid a fine of $1,200.

Improvement

Minnesota improved in 2003, finishing with a 9–7 record and nearly making the playoffs. Moss had his best season ever, catching 111 passes for 1,632 yards. He led the NFL in touchdown catches for the third time, matching his career high with 17. For the fifth time, he was chosen for the Pro Bowl.

By 2004, Minnesota quarterback Daunte Culpepper seemed fully recovered from a series of injuries. Culpepper had a great season, connecting for 39 touchdowns and 4,717 yards. He also scrambled for 800 more, setting a new NFL record for yards by a quarterback. Although Minnesota finished the regular season just 8–8, the Vikings earned a wild-card spot in the playoffs. They were scheduled to meet the Green Bay Packers in early January 2005.

For Moss, 2004 had not been a great season. He missed several games, and only managed 49 catches—less than half the number of passes he had pulled down a year earlier. On the positive side, 13 of those catches had gone for touchdowns. Could the receiver make an impact in the NFL playoffs?

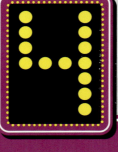

CHANGE OF SCENERY

On January 9, 2005, the Vikings faced Green Bay in an NFC wild-card playoff game. Most people expected the Packers to win. Green Bay had already beaten Minnesota twice during the 2004 season. Also, the game was being played at historic Lambeau Field, before a sold-out crowd of rowdy Green Bay fans.

Randy Moss did his best to help his team. Early in the first quarter, Moss caught a 20-yard touchdown pass to give the Vikings a 14–0 lead. By the fourth quarter, the Vikings held a 24–17 lead. Moss caught another long pass—this one 34 yards—and scored his second touchdown of the game. This locked up Minnesota's 31–17 win, enabling them to advance to the next round of the playoffs.

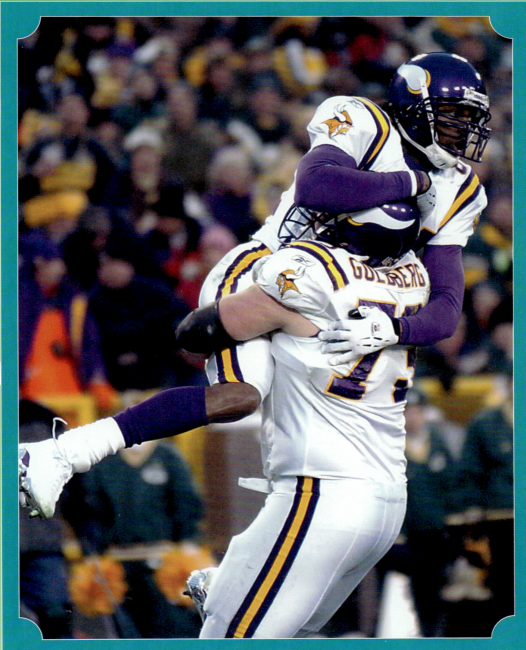

Randy Moss and offensive lineman Adam Goldberg celebrate one of Moss's two touchdown receptions in the Vikings' wild-card game against the Packers at Green Bay's Lambeau Field, January 9, 2005. Minnesota stunned Green Bay, 31–17.

While Randy Moss's churlish behavior and brushes with the law have received much press coverage, his charitable work has not been widely reported. Moss is involved in a variety of programs to help children and youth.

Moss made headlines after the game—but not for his catches, unfortunately. After his second score, the receiver had taunted the Packers' defensive backs by pretending to pull down his pants and "moon" them. The NFL fined Moss $10,000. The following week, with the Moss incident still being talked about, the Philadelphia Eagles stopped the Vikings' playoff dreams.

Controversy and Charity

By the end of 2004, Moss had scored 90 touchdowns and gained more than 9,000 yards receiving in seven NFL seasons. Many people considered him the game's most exciting wide receiver. However, Moss had become known as much for his controversial behavior as for his great catches. During Moss's career the NFL had fined him about $100,000 for his antics, while the Vikings had fined him more than $15,000.

Many people felt the receiver had a bad attitude. News stories often portrayed the star wide receiver as spoiled and arrogant.

Moss's charitable work and dedication to his community did not receive the same attention that his bad behavior did. Growing up poor in rural West Virginia, he had seen the need for youth programs. Moss spent quite a bit of his free time working with organizations such as the American Youth Football Association and the Urban Youth Racing School. These organizations are dedicated to educating young people and providing them with athletic opportunities. In addition, on Moss's days off, he sometimes visited hospitals, signing autographs and spending time with sick children.

On the Trading Block

Despite Randy Moss's extraordinary skills as a wide receiver and his dedication to community service, the Vikings' patience with their star was declining. By February 2005 Minnesota Vikings owner Red McCombs and head coach Mike Tice had seen enough. Although Moss had four years left on his contract, the Vikings were ready to let him go. They told other teams that they were willing to trade Moss.

The best offer for Moss's services came from the Oakland Raiders of the American Football Conference (AFC). The Raiders offered to trade linebacker Napoleon Harris and a seventh-round draft pick to Minnesota in exchange for Moss. Newspapers caught wind of the trade in late February 2005. When Culpepper heard that his star teammate would be leaving, he couldn't believe it:

> **"I never really thought it would happen. I wish he wasn't leaving. I really do. . . . Moss never was a negative, as far as football goes. . . . He did his thing on the field. It was the off-the-field-stuff that was negative. But he never did anything crazy that would really hurt anybody. He would do little, small things."**

After seven years and five Pro Bowls, Moss's time had ended in Minnesota. On March 2, 2005, he was officially traded to the Oakland Raiders.

Moss in Sunshine

The Oakland Raiders seemed like a good fit for Randy Moss. The team has long enjoyed a reputation as the "bad boys" of the National Football League for their tough style of play. The Raiders had once been among the NFL's best teams. They had reached the Super Bowl as recently as February 2003. Yet by 2005 Oakland was in desperate need of a playmaker. During the two seasons before Moss arrived, the team had won only nine games while losing 23.

Raiders owner Al Davis was so interested in acquiring Randy Moss that he sent two former Raiders stars to meet with the wide receiver. The two old pros—wide receiver Fred Biletnikoff and defensive back Willie Brown, both members of the Pro Football Hall of Fame—convinced Moss that the Raiders truly wanted his services.

Moss told reporters that he was sorry to leave Minnesota, but that he was excited about playing for the Raiders, a team with a great tradition of winning:

CROSS-CURRENTS

To learn more about the life and career of a great wide receiver in Oakland Raiders history, read "Fred Biletnikoff." Go to page 53. ▶▶

> **"I've still got love in Minnesota. But with the Oakland Raiders, I get a new start and a chance to go to the Super Bowl. . . . Who wouldn't want to be in the Silver and Black? I'm committed to excellence and I just want to win, baby."**

Fans pack McAfee Coliseum to see an Oakland Raiders game. The Raiders' faithful hoped that the acquisition of Randy Moss in 2005 would transform their team's offense into one of the best in the NFL.

Many experts believed that the trade would give the Raiders one of the better offenses in the league. Oakland now had two of the league's best wide receivers in Moss and Jerry Porter. In *USA Today*, writer Jarrett Bell analyzed the deal:

> **The deep passing game . . . can now be built around the league's most dangerous deep threat in Moss, who forces defenses to game plan for his presence, which opens up other areas to attack. Oakland is banking on Moss leaving his baggage in Minnesota. . . . The Raiders . . . have a history of benefiting from players who were malcontents elsewhere.**

As the team started its training camp in the summer of 2005, the question remained: Could Randy Moss stay out of trouble and help his new team?

Bad Boys

The Raiders began the 2005 season with a tough challenge: a game against the New England Patriots, who had won the two previous Super Bowls. Moss was a big part of the hard-fought game, gaining 130 yards and scoring a touchdown. However, the Patriots won the game, 30–20.

CROSS-CURRENTS

To find out more about the Raiders' bad-boy reputation, read "Appetite for Destruction: The Oakland Raiders." Go to page 54. ▸▸

The loss was a sign of things to come. Even with Moss on board, the Raiders played poorly. Although the team's offense was good, Oakland's defense was one of the worst in the NFL. It simply could not stop opponents. The Raiders finished the season with four wins and 12 losses.

Moss had several good games for the Raiders, though. In a mid-September contest against the Kansas City Chiefs, Moss caught five passes for 127 yards. One catch went for a thrilling 64-yard touchdown. On Christmas Eve of 2005, Moss reached a milestone by surpassing 10,000 yards receiving for his career. He accomplished this feat faster than all but three players in NFL history. For the year, Moss led the team in receiving with 60 catches for 1,005 yards and eight touchdowns.

After the season, the Raiders fired head coach Norv Turner. Art Shell was hired as the team's new head coach. Shell had been a Hall of Fame player for the Raiders, and had coached the team from 1989 to 1994.

Juiced Up

After the end of the 2005 season, Moss became a businessman. In June 2006 he opened a fruit juice store, Inta Juice, in his home state of West Virginia. At the grand opening of his store in Charleston, Moss donned an apron, handed out fruit smoothies, and signed autographs.

Moss's interest in selling the tasty drinks had been sparked in Minnesota two years earlier, when he and his Vikings teammates visited the franchise. On the day that his store opened, Moss clearly took pride in bringing something he enjoyed to the people of Charleston:

> **"I just think it's a good fit. We really didn't have anything here in town for the people that tasted like this and being as healthy as it is. So I just thought about investing and bringing it back home."**

The venture was also a way for Moss to improve his image, which had been tarnished by his on-the-field antics.

In 2005, after Randy Moss opened an Inta Juice store in Charleston, West Virginia, his image adorned a race car at a NASCAR event. Inta Juice is a fruit juice franchise.

Back on the Field

A few weeks after opening the Inta Juice store, Randy Moss was back on the football field at the Raiders' training camp. Although his first season with Oakland had been a disappointment, he remained optimistic. But Moss's second season began the same way that the first one had ended—with disappointing defeats.

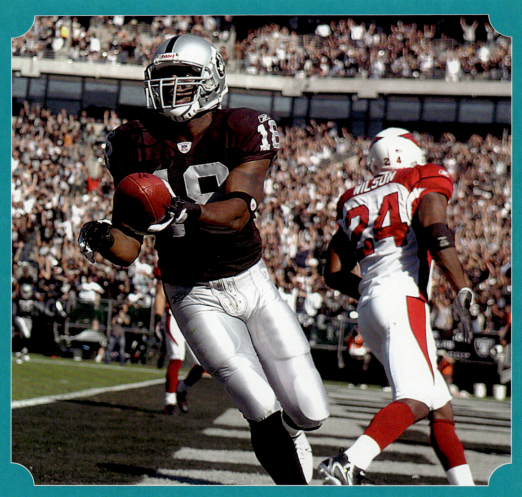

Randy Moss's 32-yard touchdown reception helped the Oakland Raiders get their first win of the 2006 season, against the Arizona Cardinals on October 22. By this time, however, the Raiders had already suffered five defeats.

In the Raiders' opening game of 2006, they lost to the San Diego Chargers, 27–0. The next week, the Baltimore Ravens walloped Oakland, 28–6. In the team's third game of the season, the Raiders quickly scored 21 points against the Cleveland Browns. But in the second half the Browns came back to win, 24–21.

In the fourth game of the season, Moss caught a 22-yard touchdown pass from quarterback Andrew Walter. It was Randy Moss's 100th career touchdown, and it gave Oakland a 13–7 lead over the San Francisco 49ers. However, the 49ers broke the game open in the second half and won easily, 34 to 20.

Oakland lost its next game as well before finally earning a win. Moss caught a 34-yard touchdown pass to help the Raiders defeat the Arizona Cardinals, 22 to 9. Although Oakland managed a second straight win the following week against the Pittsburgh Steelers, the Raiders soon returned to their losing ways. The team would not win another game for the rest of the season. Oakland finished the season with a pitiful 2–14 record. The team scored only 168 points all year.

During a mid-season loss to the Seattle Seahawks, television cameras had captured an agitated Randy Moss stewing on the bench. The trade to the Raiders had once seemed to hold such promise. Now, Moss was dejected and angry, and he wanted out of Oakland. He missed the last three games of the season due to injury, and ended the year with just 42 catches for 553 yards. He only scored three touchdowns. In an interview after the season, Moss complained about his team. This did not make Raiders players, coaches, or fans happy.

Unhappy Receiver

When Moss failed to appear at off-season training and conditioning sessions, the Raiders decided to trade their unhappy receiver to another NFL team. Only one question remained: What could the team get in return? Moss was now ranked fifth on the NFL's all-time list for career touchdown catches. However, after two subpar years he could no longer be considered one of the league's best wide receivers.

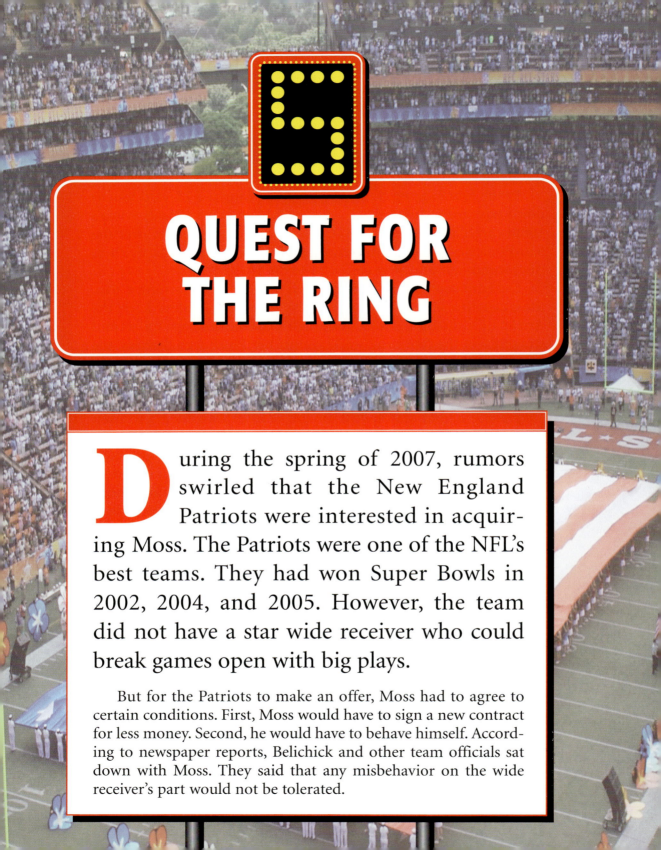

QUEST FOR THE RING

During the spring of 2007, rumors swirled that the New England Patriots were interested in acquiring Moss. The Patriots were one of the NFL's best teams. They had won Super Bowls in 2002, 2004, and 2005. However, the team did not have a star wide receiver who could break games open with big plays.

But for the Patriots to make an offer, Moss had to agree to certain conditions. First, Moss would have to sign a new contract for less money. Second, he would have to behave himself. According to newspaper reports, Belichick and other team officials sat down with Moss. They said that any misbehavior on the wide receiver's part would not be tolerated.

Randy Moss signs autographs after a training-camp practice, Foxboro, Massachusetts, July 30, 2007. "I don't think you all understand how excited I am to really be a part of this organization," the Patriots' new wide receiver told reporters.

The deal to send Randy Moss to the New England Patriots was completed on April 29, 2007. In return, Oakland received a fourth-round draft pick.

Moss signed a one-year deal with the Patriots for $3 million. This was much less than he would have earned had he stayed with the Raiders. However, Moss didn't seem to care. After two seasons with terrible teams in Oakland, Moss was happy to join a winner. He told the press,

"I don't think you all understand how excited I am to really be a part of this organization. . . . Let's put it this way: The Moss of old is back."

Many people doubted this claim. They pointed to Moss's disappointing statistics with the Raiders as evidence that the receiver's best days were behind him. Yet the Patriots were counting on Moss to return to his previous greatness. The team was anxious to return to the Super Bowl.

Something to Prove

When he arrived at New England's training camp, Randy Moss was given a locker next to the team's star quarterback, Tom Brady. The two players bonded quickly during practices and weight-lifting sessions. But the environment was a stark change for the 30-year-old Moss. Coach Belichick had a no-nonsense approach to playing football. The "Patriot Way," as players called it, was mainly about putting the team first. For most of his career, Randy Moss had the reputation of someone who put himself above the team. Now, however, Moss did his best to fit in.

During the preseason Moss was slowed by a **hamstring** injury. However, he started the season with a big game. Moss caught nine passes for 183 yards and a touchdown. He averaged more than 20 yards per catch as New England easily beat the New York Jets, 38–14.

Moss gained more than 100 yards receiving in each of the team's first four games. In a game against the Buffalo Bills, Moss bolted 45 yards down the sideline to catch up with a Brady bomb. Moss proved that he was still among the fastest players in the NFL, blowing past much younger defensive backs. He also used his six-foot-four height to reach balls that few other receivers could grab.

As Moss racked up great statistics and helped his team win each week, sportswriters noted that the receiver had mellowed. He no longer pouted when things didn't go his way. Instead, he encouraged teammates and was often spotted chatting with Tom Brady on the bench when New England's defense was on the field.

A Huge Year for Moss

Midway through the season, Randy Moss had caught 47 passes for 779 yards and 11 touchdowns. This put him among the league leaders in all three categories. His catches had helped the team win its first eight games.

In the season's ninth week, New England faced a tough test: a game in Indianapolis against the defending Super Bowl champions. The Colts, led by quarterback Peyton Manning, were also unbeaten. Moss had one of his best games, catching nine passes for 145 yards

Randy Moss runs a pattern during practice, 2007. As the 2007 season progressed, sportswriters noticed a different Randy Moss, one who seemed to have bought into the Patriots' team-first philosophy.

and a touchdown. One catch went for 55 yards. In the end, the Patriots won a close game, 24–20, to keep their perfect season alive. Afterward, Colts coach Tony Dungy said,

> **"We didn't have the answer for Randy Moss today. We had a lot of attention paid to him trying to stop him from catching the deep balls but he caught the deep one at the big time of the game. That was really the play of the game, got [the Patriots] a quick score."**

Indianapolis defensive back Antoine Bethea interferes with Randy Moss on a long pass play during the Colts-Patriots showdown of November 4, 2007. Moss had a huge game, and New England won, 24–20, to remain undefeated.

Only one team in NFL history had ever finished a season without a loss—the 1972 Miami Dolphins. In those days teams played 14 games, not 16, during the regular season. As the Patriots continued winning, people began to wonder if they could be the first team to go undefeated in a 16-game season.

Moss continued to do his part to help his team win. In New England's next game, a rematch against Buffalo, Moss caught 10 passes and scored four touchdowns. The receiver continued to put up big numbers as the Patriots kept winning. He caught two touchdowns—one on a 63-yard touchdown pass—in a win over Pittsburgh.

CROSS-CURRENTS

To learn more about the first team to complete an NFL season without a loss, read "Undefeated Dolphins." Go to page 55. ▶▶

The pressure was for the team's final game, against the New York Giants. If New England could win, it would complete the undefeated season. Early in the second quarter, Moss caught a four-yard touchdown pass to give the Patriots a 10–7 advantage. By the fourth quarter, the Giants had battled back to take a 28–23 lead. Then Moss scored on a 65-yard pass from Tom Brady. New England made the **two-point conversion** to go ahead, 31–28. Moss finished with six catches for 100 yards and the Patriots made NFL history with a 38–35 victory.

Moss himself made history in the team's final game. His first score had tied the league's record for touchdown catches in a season. His second touchdown of the game was his 23rd of the season. This set a new NFL mark. Moss finished the regular season with 98 catches for 1,493 yards. Now, the receiver had to get ready for the playoffs.

Road to the Super Bowl

On January 12, 2008, the Patriots met the Jacksonville Jaguars in an AFC divisional playoff game. It was cold and blustery—perfect football weather—and Gillette Stadium in Foxboro, Massachusetts, was packed with Patriots fans waving their red, white, and blue. Tom Brady lit up the sky with a series of perfect passes. Although Moss had only one reception, Brady completed 26 of 28 passes, breaking an NFL record. The Patriots beat the Jaguars, 31–20, and moved on to the AFC Championship.

Jacksonville Jaguars quarterback David Garrard (#9) has good protection on this pass play against the New England Patriots in the AFC divisional playoffs, January 12, 2008. But New England ultimately shut down the Jaguars, winning 31–20.

On paper, the San Diego Chargers posed a challenge. However, the Chargers proved to be no match for the Patriots' defense. San Diego managed just four field goals. Although Moss was hardly a factor in the game, and Brady threw three interceptions, the Patriots won easily, 21–12. New England was headed to the Super Bowl for the fourth time in seven years.

Unfortunately, an off-field issue distracted Moss. During the playoffs, a Florida woman accused Moss of beating her up. Moss denied the woman's account. He said that she was simply trying to get money from him.

The NFL's Biggest Game

After almost 10 years in the NFL, Randy Moss had finally reached the Super Bowl. He told reporters that he felt prepared to play in the biggest game of his life.

CROSS-CURRENTS

Read "Spygate" to learn about an issue that dogged the Patriots during their run to Super Bowl XLII. Go to page 56. ▶▶

The Patriots' regular season and playoff dominance made them strong favorites. Their opponent in Super Bowl XLII would be the team they had beaten at the end of the regular season, the New York Giants. The Giants had won three tough playoff games on the road to reach the Super Bowl. However, few people felt they had a chance against the Patriots. Their quarterback, Eli Manning, had yet to fully prove his ability. He had often been criticized for his poor play in big games.

Patriots quarterback Tom Brady, on the other hand, had a well-deserved reputation for being calm under fire. He had led the Patriots to victories even when the team was struggling. In 2007 Brady had thrown an NFL-record 50 touchdown passes. He helped New England set a new NFL record by scoring 589 points. This broke the record that Moss and the Vikings had set back in 1998.

Ready to Play

When the Super Bowl began, both teams came out ready to play. The Giants took the first kickoff and then used 10 minutes of the game clock, settling eventually for a field goal. As the first quarter ended, the Patriots made it to the Giants' one-yard line and soon after scored the first touchdown of the game. But the Giants' pass rush kept Brady in check, forcing him to rush throws or run to avoid sacks. Brady couldn't energize his team's high-scoring offense. The teams went to the locker room separated by only four points, with the Patriots up, 7–3.

Early in the fourth quarter, Eli Manning found receiver David Tyree in the end zone to make the score 10–7 in favor of the Giants. But the Patriots didn't panic. Instead, they marched 80 yards down the field. With less than three minutes left in the game, Brady hit

Randy Moss's six-yard touchdown reception put New England up by a score of 14–10 late in the fourth quarter of Super Bowl XLII. But the New York Giants would come back to score with just 35 seconds left in the game, upsetting the heavily favored Patriots, 17–14.

Moss with a six-yard touchdown pass. With a 14-10 lead, it seemed the Patriots would win their fourth Super Bowl.

Giants quarterback Eli Manning had other ideas, however. He led his team on a 12-play, 83-yard drive. With only 35 seconds left in the game, Manning fired a 13-yard pass into the end zone. New York's Plaxico Burress caught the pass for a touchdown. There was not enough time for the Patriots to make another comeback. They lost the game, 17–14.

What the Future Holds

Despite the disappointing loss, Moss voiced a desire to remain with the team until his retirement. The Patriots were interested in bringing the big receiver back. On March 3, 2008, New England signed Moss to a three-year, $27 million deal.

Randy Moss has already established himself as one of the greatest wide receivers in NFL history. He is among the league's all-time leaders in career **receiving yards** and touchdown catches. Only time will tell whether Moss can achieve the one goal that has eluded him so far: winning a Super Bowl ring.

Coach Belichick

Bill Belichick of the Patriots has coached longer than any other active coach, with 33 years in the NFL. Patriots fans know him as a man who praises opposing teams, downplays his own team's successes, and rarely smiles during games or press conferences. These things are all part of a strategy he uses to keep players motivated. He knows that if expectations are high, they can work in a rival team's favor. He's been praised for his ability to extract the best performance from his squads.

Belichick was born in Nashville, Tennessee, on April 16, 1952. He was raised in Annapolis, Maryland. Football ran in his family. His father, Steve, played fullback for the Detroit Lions and later coached at the Naval Academy. Bill was an outstanding player at the high school level, and he is honored in Annapolis High's Hall of Fame. He went to college at Wesleyan, and earned a degree in economics in 1975.

Belichick worked as an assistant coach for the Baltimore Colts, Detroit Lions and Denver Broncos. For 12 years, he was an assistant coach with the New York Giants, working with both defense and special teams, before being named defensive coordinator in 1985. Belichick's first opportunity as a head coach came in 1991, when he took over the Cleveland Browns. However, his time there was largely disappointing. In five seasons, the Browns managed just a 36–44 record. Belichick also angered fans when he cut popular quarterback Bernie Kosar in 1993, replacing him with Vinny Testaverde. Belichick ended his career with the Browns during dark days for Cleveland fans. After the team finished 5–11 in 1995, owner Art Modell moved the franchise to Baltimore.

After being fired by the franchise (now the Baltimore Ravens) in 1996, Belichick held several assistant coaching jobs. In 2000, he was hired as the Patriots' head coach. Since then, Belichick has established himself as one of the best coaches in the NFL. His teams won three Super Bowls in four years. The Patriots have also set several records for win streaks, including consecutive overall wins (21), consecutive regular season wins (18), and consecutive playoff wins.

After joining the Patriots in 2007, Randy Moss told reporters how much he admired the head coach:

❝ Coach Belichick is a [great] coach, if not the greatest ever, and I really mean that. . . . Coach Belichick has a tight grasp on us; he doesn't let us get too ahead of ourselves. At the same time, he lets us enjoy what we're doing. **❞**

(Go back to page 5.) ◀◀

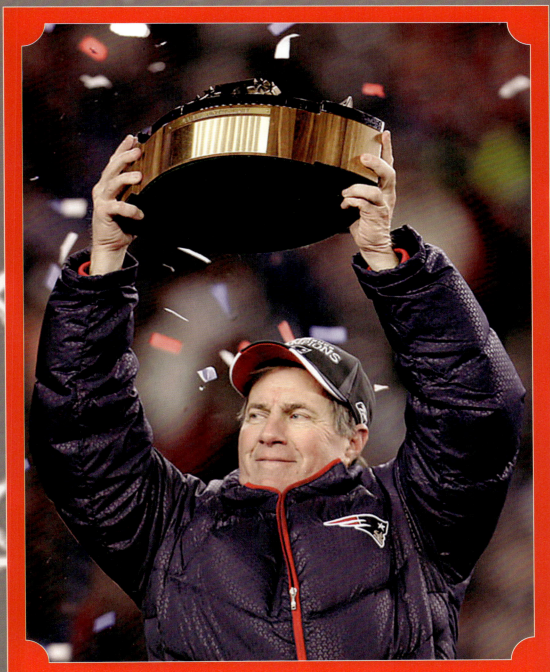

New England Patriots head coach Bill Belichick holds up the Lamar Hunt AFC Championship Trophy after his team's 21–12 victory over the San Diego Chargers, January 20, 2008. Belichick has coached the Patriots to three Super Bowl victories.

The New England Patriots

With quarterback Tom Brady (#12) in front, the New England Patriots await their introduction before a game. The Patriots have been one of the NFL's most successful teams in recent years, winning Super Bowls in 2002, 2004, and 2005.

The New England Patriots faced many difficult years before the team finally gained success. The Patriots came into existence in 1959, when a group of local businessmen led by William H. "Billy" Sullivan Jr. succeeded in having the Boston-based club accepted into the American Football League (AFL). It was the eighth and last team admitted into the AFL, one of two professional football leagues in America at the time. A public contest was held to name the squad, which first played as the Boston Patriots.

The Patriots played their first games at Boston University Field. Lou Saban was the team's first head coach. A Patriots defensive player, Bob Dee, recovered a fumble and scored the team's first touchdown in a game against the Buffalo Bills. Throughout the 1960s, the Patriots produced outstanding players but did not earn a championship. In 1969, the AFL merged with the National Football League and the Patriots became an NFL squad in the American Football Conference.

The Patriots barely had a home in their first decade. They moved from Boston University Field to Harvard Stadium, Fenway Park, and Boston College Alumni Stadium. In 1970, the team moved from Boston to Foxboro. The next year, the team's name was changed to the New England Patriots.

During the 1970s and 1980s, the Patriots never won a championship, although the team continued to produce its share of stars. One of these was John Hannah, an offensive tackle who was eventually elected to the Pro Football Hall of Fame. In 1978, the Patriots won the first division title in their history, but lost to the Houston Oilers in their first home playoff game. In 1985, New England won its first trip to the Super Bowl. However, their opponent was the powerful Chicago Bears, considered one of the greatest NFL teams of all time. The Bears routed the Patriots, 46–10. At the time, this was the most one-sided game in Super Bowl history.

In January 1994, Robert K. Kraft became the team's fourth owner. He promised fans that the Patriots would win a championship within 10 years. The Patriots delivered on that promise in 2002, when they defeated the heavily favored Rams in the Super Bowl. The Patriots delivered two more Super Bowl victories in the next three years, with wins over the Carolina Panthers (2004) and the Philadelphia Eagles (2005). With Randy Moss on the team, the Patriots were favored to win another Super Bowl in 2008, but they were upset by the New York Giants.

(Go back to page 9.) ◄◄

Notre Dame: A Proud Football History

The University of Notre Dame in northern Indiana is a Catholic university with a respected academic reputation. However, on Saturdays each fall the books are put away as 81,000 Fighting Irish football fans fill Notre Dame Stadium to the rafters.

The school's proud football tradition began modestly in 1887, when Notre Dame lost its first game to Michigan. Ups and downs followed until Knute Rockne took over the head coaching duties. During his tenure (1918–1930), the Irish won three national championships, posting 105 wins, 12 losses, and five ties.

During the 1940s, one of Rockne's former star players, Frank Leahy, took over as the team's coach. During his 11 seasons, the Fighting Irish won four national championships and had six undefeated seasons.

After Leahy retired, the Fighting Irish continued to be one of the nation's top college football programs, winning national titles in 1966, 1973, 1977, and 1988. Overall, Notre Dame's football teams have won over 800 games. Seven of Notre Dame's players have won the Heisman Trophy, and 10 former Irish players are members of the Pro Football Hall of Fame, including former San Francisco 49ers quarterback Joe Montana. (Go back to page 11.) ◄◄

The Heisman Trophy

The Heisman Trophy is given to the country's best college football player each year. It is generally considered the most prestigious award a college football player can receive.

The award is presented each December, after the regular college games have ended but before the major bowl games. Any college football player is eligible, but the winners usually come from the high-profile NCAA Division I schools that compete for the national championship and play in the major bowls. Sportswriters from all over the country, along with former winners of the award, get to vote. In addition, there is a fan vote that is taken into account. Voters select three players, with three points awarded to the top choice, two for second, and one for third. The player with the most points is the Heisman winner.

The award is named for John W. Heisman (1869–1936), a famous coach from the early history of football. Heisman developed a number of plays and formations still in use today. While the coach of Georgia Tech in 1916, his team crushed the Cumberland College Bulldogs, 222–0. This was the most lopsided game in college football history. Heisman later served as director of New York City's Downtown Athletic Club (DAC). In 1935, this organization began awarding a trophy to the best college football player. After Heisman's death the next year, the trophy was renamed in his honor.

The Heisman Trophy is one of the most recognizable awards in sports. It was created by noted sculptor Frank Eliscu. He used a New York University football star named Ed Smith as a model. His finished bronze sculpture featured a player running with the ball, arm outstretched to ward off tacklers.

Winning the Heisman Trophy does not ensure that a player will succeed in the NFL. In fact, many Heisman winners have not had great pro careers. A few Heisman winners who did succeed include Dallas Cowboys Hall of Fame quarterback Roger Staubach, explosive Detroit Lions running back Barry Sanders, and the versatile Reggie Bush of the New Orleans Saints.

In 1997, Randy Moss was selected as one of 10 finalists for the Heisman Trophy. This was a great honor for a second-year player. In the final voting for the trophy, he finished fourth with 253 points, including 17 first-place votes. Charles Woodson of Michigan won the award with 1,815 points, followed by quarterback Peyton Manning of Tennessee and quarterback Ryan Leaf of Washington State.

(Go back to page 15.) ◀◀

The Pro Bowl

The idea to gather the best players in the NFL at the end of the year for an all-star game first came about in 1938. The game, however, didn't become an annual event until 1951. This game was known as the Pro All-Star Game until 1970, when the American Football League (AFL) merged with the National Football League. It was then renamed the Pro Bowl.

The Pro Bowl is played every year in February, one week after the Super Bowl, the game that determines the NFL champion. Since 1980, the Pro Bowl has been held at Aloha Stadium in Honolulu, Hawaii, which ensures a warm climate and an enjoyable experience for the fans as well as the players and their families.

Until 1995, the Pro Bowl participants were chosen by a vote of NFL players and coaches. Since that time, the fans have been given the chance to help select players. The votes of the fans, players, and coaches are all weighed equally in determining who will represent the AFC and NFC in the game. All voters are expected to choose the players who have enjoyed the best seasons.

The Pro Bowl does not feature the rough play of a regular-season game. It is generally more of a fun game than a competitive experience for the players. The players' goals are not only to win the game, but also to prevent getting injured or injuring others. The intensity of the play typically doesn't pick up until the fourth quarter, when the game's outcome hangs in the balance.

The game often features wide-open offenses and a great deal of passing, which makes it more enjoyable for both the fans in the stadium and the people watching at home on television. The teams usually score many touchdowns. Since 2000, the winning Pro Bowl team has tallied 31 points or more in eight of the nine games.

Though the players on the winning team receive a little more money for their efforts, the outcome of the game is not considered very important to most participants and fans. Neither the NFC nor the AFC has proven dominant in the Pro Bowl for a long period of time. Since 1981, neither team has ever won more than three games in a row.

For NFL players, it is an honor to be selected to play in the Pro Bowl. During his career, Randy Moss has been chosen for six Pro Bowls, in 1998, 1999, 2000, 2002, 2003, and 2007.

(Go back to page 19.)

Head Coach Dennis Green

By the time Randy Moss joined the Minnesota Vikings in 1998, Dennis Green had established a reputation as one of the top coaches in the National Football League. After becoming the Vikings head coach in 1992, Green posted winning records every year. But when Moss arrived, the Vikings emerged as one of the NFL's best teams. Green's 15-1 record with the Vikings in 1998 is one of the best records of any team in the history of the league. It earned him Coach of the Year honors from *Sports Illustrated* magazine.

Green played college football at the University of Iowa, where he was a tailback and flanker. After graduating from Iowa in 1971, he played a year of professional football with the British Columbia Lions of the Canadian Football League. Green then became a coach. He

In 13 seasons as an NFL head coach, Dennis Green compiled a record of 113 wins and 94 losses. He spent 10 years coaching the Minnesota Vikings and 3 years coaching the Arizona Cardinals.

gained valuable experience as an assistant coach at the University of Iowa, the University of Dayton, and Stanford University.

In 1981, Green became the second African-American head coach in Division I-A history when he took the job at Northwestern University. He was named the Big Ten Conference Coach of the Year the next season. In 1985, Green left college football to coach in the NFL. Green worked as running-backs coach for the San Francisco 49ers under head coach Bill Walsh. In 1989, Green returned to college football as head coach for Stanford University. He remained at Stanford until he got the job as coach of the Minnesota Vikings on January 10, 1992. Green became the third African-American head coach in NFL history, after Fritz Pollard (who coached in the 1920s) and Art Shell (who coached the Oakland Raiders from 1989 to 1994).

Although Green regularly reached the playoffs with Minnesota, the team could never break through to the Super Bowl. He was fired after the 2001 season—his first in the NFL with a losing record. As head coach of the Vikings, Green had a record of 97 wins and 62 losses for a winning percentage of .610.

In 2004, Dennis Green was hired as the coach of the Arizona Cardinals. However, he was unable to turn the franchise around. He was fired in 2006 after three losing seasons. Today, Green is working as a television analyst. His autobiography, *No Room for Crybabies*, was published in 1997. (Go back to page 19.) ◄◄

Fred Biletnikoff

Fred Biletnikoff, who encouraged Randy Moss to play for the Oakland Raiders, was an All-Pro wide receiver in the 1960s and 1970s. Born in Erie, Pennsylvania, in 1943, Biletnikoff starred in college for the Florida State University Seminoles. He was an All-American in 1964. Biletnikoff ended his college career in spectacular fashion. Playing against the University of Oklahoma in the Gator Bowl, Biletnikoff helped the Seminoles to victory with four touchdown catches.

The Oakland Raiders drafted Biletnikoff with the second overall pick in the 1965 NFL draft. Although he did not get a chance to play regularly until 1967, Biletnikoff made the most of his opportunity and kept his place as a starter until he retired in 1978. Biletnikoff earned All-Pro honors in 1972. He played in two Super Bowls and was named Most Valuable Player (MVP) in the Raiders' 32–14 win over the Minnesota Vikings in Super Bowl XI.

At the time he retired, Biletnikoff's total of 589 receptions placed him fourth on the all-time list. The catches were good for 8,974 yards and 76 touchdowns. In 1988, Biletnikoff was inducted into the Pro Football Hall of Fame. Three years later, he was inducted into the College Football Hall of Fame. In 1994, the Tallahassee Quarterback Club created the Biletnikoff Award, which is presented each year to the best receiver in college football. (Go back to page 30.) ◄◄

Appetite for Destruction: The Oakland Raiders

During the 1970s, the Oakland Raiders gained a reputation as the bad boys of the National Football League. The team's owner, Al Davis, wanted his black-and-silver team to be feared—and to win. The bad boys of professional football lived by Davis's motto: "Just win, baby." The Raiders lived up to their name. "When they came to town," said former Philadelphia Eagle Herman Edwards, "they acted like they wanted to burn the whole village down."

The idea, explained former Oakland cornerback Lester Hayes, was to get into the heads of opponents and intimidate them. Although the Raiders' offense could post big numbers on the scoreboard, it was the defense that scared opponents. Hayes learned the ropes from Pro Bowlers Jack "the Assassin" Tatum, Willie Brown, and George Atkinson. The three were known as brutal tacklers who bragged about their ability to hurt receivers who crossed their paths. In 1978 Tatum hit Patriots wide receiver Daryl Stingley so hard that Stingley was paralyzed for the rest of his life.

The Raiders gained a reputation for winning at all costs—even if that meant cheating. The players slathered Stickum, a

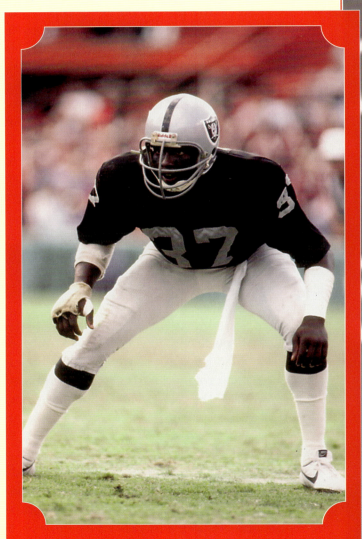

In his 10-year career with the Raiders (1977–1986), cornerback Lester Hayes gained a reputation as a fierce hitter. The Raiders of his era were known as one of the NFL's toughest—and dirtiest—teams.

brown, sticky substance, on their shirts, their hands, and even their helmets so the football would stick to them like a fly on flypaper. Stickum helped Lester Hayes win the NFL Defensive Player of the Year award in 1980 after he intercepted 13 passes. After that season, NFL officials banned Stickum because it gave defenders an unfair advantage.

Offensive tackle Bob Brown worked at gaining an on-field advantage in another way. He persuaded the NFL to allow him to use wrist braces for protection. What he failed to mention was that the braces were made of hard leather and covered his whole hand. When a play started, he would take two steps back and then drive his heavy hands into the pass rusher's chest. Opponents described Brown's wrist guards as weapons. The NFL agreed and forced Brown to add rubber padding to the guards.

The Raiders' players and coaches used a variety of tricks and tactics to unsettle and intimidate opposing players. As a result, the tough Raiders won Super Bowls in 1977, 1981, and 1984. The team reached the Super Bowl after the 2002 season, but lost badly to the Tampa Bay Buccaneers. Since then, however, the Raiders have struggled, with five straight losing seasons. (Go back to page 32.) ◀◀

Undefeated Dolphins

The 1972 Miami Dolphins are the only team in NFL history to go undefeated for an entire season. At the time, NFL teams played 14 games, rather than the 16 that are played today. Miami won all of its regular-season games, two playoff games, and Super Bowl VII.

Coach Don Shula was in his third year as Miami's head coach when the Dolphins' run began. Their team had many star players. Quarterback Bob Griese went on to the Hall of Fame, as did Larry Csonka, Larry Little, Nick Buoniconti, Jim Langer, and Paul Warfield. But the Dolphins also had many role players. Miami's defensive unit was nicknamed the "No-Name Defense" because so many lesser-known players made big plays.

Quarterback Earl Morrall became part of the legend when he came off the bench to replace an injured Griese in the fifth week of the season. Morrall was 38, very old by the standards of professional football. But he kept the streak alive through the rest of the season, and won a playoff game against Cleveland. The next week, Griese returned to lead the Dolphins past the Pittsburgh Steelers. The Dolphins finished their historic journey with a 14–7 triumph over the Washington Redskins in Super Bowl VII.

(Go back to page 41.) ◀◀

Spygate

In 2007 an event that occurred early in the Patriots' run toward an undefeated regular season became a national controversy. It was called "Spygate" by the media and threatened the team's ability to stay focused on winning a championship.

In their 2007 season opener, the Patriots crushed the Jets, 38–14. The victory was not a surprise. New England had been favored to win. But after the game, Jets officials complained to the league that a member of the Patriots staff had violated NFL rules. The Patriots had sent someone to the sidelines to videotape the Jets' coaching staff's defensive signals during the game. The Jets had confronted the assistant and confiscated his camera during the game.

When this evidence was revealed, the National Football League officially charged the Patriots with breaking the rules. The league fined Coach Belichick $500,000, fined the Patriots another $250,000, and stripped the team of a first-round pick in the 2008 draft. Belichick's fine was the highest ever imposed on a coach.

The media began to refer to the incident as "Spygate." The name came from "Watergate," the name of the Washington hotel burglarized by men working for President Richard Nixon in 1972, as they attempted to put eavesdropping equipment in his political opponents' headquarters. The scandal that resulted as the involvement of Nixon's men was uncovered forced the president to resign in disgrace in 1974. Since then, the press has often added the term "-gate" to public scandals.

Few fans or reporters considered the videotaping a major factor in the Patriots' success, but it was a serious violation of the rules. Two days after the game, Belichick issued a public apology. He said that the taping had no effect on the outcome of the game against the Jets, however, and declared he would not make any other statement about it. Patriots owner Robert Kraft also apologized publicly. Later, both men apologized privately at meetings of NFL coaches and team owners.

After apologizing, Belichick tried to turn the incident to his team's advantage. All the controversy, he told the players, just demonstrated that the media was out to get New England. This proved to be a very effective strategy—typical of Belichick's motivation techniques—and it helped the Patriots return their focus to winning games. However, many fans were shocked by the charges. In the weeks before the Super Bowl, the media reported extensively on the spying controversy.

(Go back to page 43.)

1977 Randall Gene Moss is born in Rand, West Virginia, on February 13.

1995 Moss pleads guilty to attacking a fellow high school student, and loses his scholarship to the University of Notre Dame.

1996 In his first year at Marshall University, Moss sets records for most games with a touchdown (14) and most consecutive games with a touchdown catch (13); Marshall wins Division I-AA championship.

1997 Moss catches 25 touchdown passes for Marshall, and finishes fourth in Heisman Trophy voting.

1998 The Minnesota Vikings choose Moss as the 21st pick in the NFL draft; the Vikings finish 15–1 but lose the NFC Championship to the Atlanta Falcons. Moss is named to the Pro Bowl and receives Offensive Rookie of the Year award, with a rookie record 17 touchdown catches.

1999 In his second year with the Vikings, Moss catches 80 passes and scores 11 touchdowns. During a playoff loss to the St. Louis Rams, Moss squirts a referee with water and is fined by the NFL.

2000 Moss is selected for his third Pro Bowl, finishing with 77 catches for 1,437 yards and a league-leading 15 touchdowns.

2001 Moss becomes the NFL's highest-paid player when he and the Vikings agree on an eight-year, $75 million contract.

2002 Moss is arrested for bumping a police officer with his car; during the incident, police find marijuana. Eventually, Moss pleads guilty to a minor violation; he serves 40 hours of community service and pays a $12,000 fine.

2004 During a wild-card playoff game against the Green Bay Packers, Moss pretends to "moon" his opponents after scoring a touchdown; he is later fined $10,000 for the incident.

2005 In February the Vikings trade Moss to the Oakland Raiders for linebacker Napoleon Harris and two seventh-round draft choices; the Raiders finish with a record of 4–12.

2006 In June Moss opens his first business, a franchise named Inta Juice. The Raiders and Moss have another lackluster year, winning only two games.

2007 In April the Raiders trade Moss to the New England Patriots, receiving a fourth-round draft pick in return. During the season, Moss sets a record for most touchdown catches by a wide receiver, with 23.

2008 The New York Giants defeat the Patriots in Super Bowl XLII. Moss signs a three-year contract with New England.

Career Statistics

Season	Team	G	Rec	Yds	Avg	Lng	TD
1998	Min	16	69	1,313	19.0	61T	17
1999	Min	16	80	1,413	17.7	67T	11
2000	Min	16	77	1,437	18.7	78T	15
2001	Min	16	82	1,233	15.0	73T	10
2002	Min	16	106	1,347	12.7	60	7
2003	Min	16	111	1,632	14.7	72	17
2004	Min	13	49	767	15.7	82T	13
2005	Oak	16	60	1,005	16.8	79	8
2006	Oak	13	42	553	13.2	51	3
2007	NE	16	98	1,493	15.2	65T	23
Total		154	774	12,193	15.8	82	124

Awards and Records

Fred Biletnikoff Award, 1997

NFL Offensive Rookie of the Year Award, 1998

All-Pro First Team selection, 1998, 2000, 2003, 2007

Pro Bowl selection, 1998, 1999, 2000, 2002, 2003, 2007

NFL rookie record: 17 touchdown catches in a season, 1998

NFL record: 23 touchdown catches in a season, 2007

Books

Bernstein, Ross. *Randy Moss: Star Wide Receiver*. Berkeley Heights, N.J.: Enslow, 2002.

Miller, Calvin Craig. *Tom Brady*. Philadelphia: Mason Crest Publishers, 2009.

Stewart, Mark. *Randy Moss: First in Flight*. Minneapolis: Millbrook Press, 2000.

Temple, Bob. *Randy Moss*. Minneapolis: A Child's World, 2001.

Thornley, Stew. *Randy Moss*. Berkeley Heights, N.J.: Enslow, 2003.

Web Sites

www.therealrandymoss.com

The Internet home of the All-Pro wide receiver is chock full of photographs, videos, and interviews. Highlights also include information on Moss's charity work with children.

www.nfl.com

This is the official Web site of the National Football League. Besides the latest scores and statistics, the site contains a page on every team and pro player. Read about this season's draft or download interviews with the game's movers and shakers.

www.patriots.com

Catch up on the latest news about the New England Patriots by surfing over to this Web site. Look up the new season schedule; vote your favorite retired Patriots into the Hall of Fame; and more.

www.mosszone.com

This fan site is chock full of videos and statistics relating to Randy Moss. It includes a running list of Moss news stories, as well as a forum on which fans can post comments about their favorite wide receiver.

www.randymossmotorsports.com

Randy Moss is fast, but his trucks are faster. The Pro Bowl wide receiver's latest venture is the formation of a NASCAR truck team, which will compete across the country beginning in the summer of 2008. The Web site tells all about it.

contract—an agreement between two parties. In the NFL, these agreements are between players and teams and involve decisions on how many years the player will play for a specific team and how much the team will pay the player.

draft—the National Football League's annual selection of new players, usually from colleges and universities.

drive—the series of plays an offense uses to attempt to score, either with a field goal or a touchdown.

free agent—a professional athlete who is not under contract to any team. This allows the player to sign the best contract he is offered.

gridiron—a field marked with parallel white lines, on which football is played.

hamstring—any of the muscles that surround the back of the knee.

negotiation—to talk with another person or group to settle a matter or disagreement.

postseason—a synonym for the NFL playoffs.

receiving yards—the number of yards covered on the field during a completed forward pass.

reception—in football, a forward pass that is caught by a member of the offensive team.

rookie—a first-year player on a team.

scholarship—money awarded to a student-athlete to help with educational costs and living expenses.

two-point conversion—an opportunity for a team to score two points after a touchdown. The team that scored a touchdown can try to run or pass the ball into the end zone from the two-yard line. If a player can reach the end zone with the ball, the team is awarded two extra points.

wild card—one of the two playoff berths in each of the NFL's conferences awarded to a team that has not won its division but that has a better record than the remaining teams.

wide receiver—a football player whose primary job is to catch passes.

page 7 "In this case . . ." Mark Maske, "Moss Likes the Position He's In," *Washington Post* (January 30, 2008), p. E1.

page 9 "Before I retired . . . " Maske, "Moss Likes the Position He's In," p. E1.

page 10 "After God is . . ." *The Moss Method: It's a Way of Life*, Allumination FilmWorks LLC, 2006.

page 12 "It was a bad scene . . ." Jackie MacMullan, "Moss's Blessing, and Curse," *Boston Globe* (January 20, 2008). http://www.boston.com/sports/football/patriots/articles/2008/01/20/mosss_blessing_and_curse/?page=3.

page 19 "I saw in Randy . . ." David Scott, "Moss Hysteria," *Sport* 90, no. 8 (August 1999), p. 50.

page 22 "I've been waiting . . ." Mike Whiteford, "Moss Deal: Eight Years, $75 Million," *Charleston Gazette* (July 26, 2001), p. C1.

page 30 "I never really thought . . ." Sean Jensen, "Moss Traded, Agent Says," *St. Paul Pioneer Press* (February 24, 2005), p. A1.

page 30 "I've still got love . . ." Associated Press, "Raiders Complete Trade for Prolific Receiver," ESPN.com (March 3, 2005). http://sports.espn.go.com/nfl/news/story?id=2003487

page 31 "The deep passing game . . ." Jarrett Bell, "Volatile Moss Makes Raiders More Explosive," *USA Today* (March 3, 2005), p. C2.

page 33 "I just think . . ." John Raby, "Randy Moss Opens Fruit-Juice Franchise," *Star Tribune* (June 29, 2006). http://www.startribune.com/sports/vikings/11703821.html.

page 38 "I don't think . . ." Dennis Dillon, "Pushing the Limit," *Sporting News*, May 7, 2007.

page 40 "We didn't have the answer . . ." Associated Press, "Manning's Late Fumble Seals Deal for Undefeated Patriots." ESPN.com (November 4, 2007). http://sports.espn.go.com/nfl/recap?gameId=271104011

page 46 "Coach Belichick is . . ." Mike Reiss and Christopher L. Gasper, "Moss Has Praise for Belichick," *Boston Globe* (October 15, 2007). http://www.boston.com/sports/football/patriots/articles/2007/10/15/moss_has_praise_for_belichick/

page 54 "When they came to town . . ." Jeffri Chadlha, "Notorious Image Sticks With These Raiders," ESPN.com (August 9, 2007). http://sports.espn.go.com/espn/cheat/news/story?id=2957892

Numbers in **bold italics** refer to captions.

David Robson is an award-winning writer and English professor. He is the recipient of a National Endowment for the Arts grant and two playwriting fellowships from the Delaware Division of the Arts. An avid football fan since boyhood, David's gridiron heroes include Hall of Fame quarterback Terry Bradshaw. David lives with his wife and daughter in Wilmington, Delaware.

PICTURE CREDITS

page

5: The Boston Globe/SPCS
6: Ben Laing/AASI Photos
8: Kristen Martin/AASI Photos
11: Dan Honda/Contra Costa Times/KRT
13: NEP/PRMS
14: T&T/IOA Photos
17: Fleer/NMI
18: John Doman/St. Paul Pioneer Press/KRT
20: NFL/Wirelmage
23: Jim Gehrz/St. Paul Pioneer Press/KRT
24: Sports Illustrated/NMI
27: John Doman/St. Paul Pioneer Press/KRT
28: Ray M./CIC Photos

31: G. Pulido/AASI Photos
33: Cobby17/AASI Photos
34: John Green/Cal Sport Media
37: NEP/PRMS
39: Nathan Wood/SPCS
40: dadart/AASI Photos
42: Victoria Welch/SPCS
44: NFL/SPCS
47: Steven Frischling/MCT
48: NEP/SPCS
52: Jim Gehrz/Minneapolis Star Tribune/MCT
54: J. Warren/NFL/SPCS

Front cover: The Boston Globe/SPCS
Front cover inset: Elsa/Getty Images